DEADLY JAMES

and Other Poems

DEADLY JAMES

and Other Poems

by

James A. Emanuel

Illustrated by
Nicole Lamotte

Lotus Press
Detroit
1987

International Standard Book Number 0-916418-67-7
Library of Congress Catalog Card Number 87-81853

Manufactured in the United States of America

Lotus Press, Inc.
Post Office Box 21607
Detroit, Michigan 48221

To Julia,
  Gladys, and
  Christine, my sisters
  and Ray, my brother

Poetry by James A. Emanuel:

The Treehouse and Other Poems
Panther Man
Black Man Abroad: The Toulouse Poems
A Chisel in the Dark (Poems Selected and New)
A Poet's Mind
The Broken Bowl (New and Collected Poems)
Deadly James and Other Poems

Preface

This book, from its opening picture of man struggling to cut away his own "False Notions" to its closing portrait of a "Poet as Fisherman" casting for a masterpiece, reflects desperation and optimism common to authors. Similar extremes—and the historical function of poetry-writing in handling them—have at times been unforgettably recorded. We remember, for example, Etheridge Knight's straightforward "I died in 1960 from a prison sentence & poetry brought me back to life." And students of 18th century British poetry never blot out the self-image of troubled William Cowper (the deer "long stricken from the herd"), who wrote "My soul lay out of sight, / untuned, unstrung."

The order in which the poems of this book were written (in Paris, 1984-1986, with two exceptions) is approximately preserved in the seven sections, individually and as a whole. Thus the shifting themes portray the tug-of-war progression from the near-extinction of creativity to its re-emergence. The focal "Deadly James" appears near enough to the midpoint of the chronology to bring hindsight, revealing an undercurrent of unremitting force and changing direction. This unconscious interplay behind each poem, moving toward and away from that focal poem, is patterned in each book section: beginning with transitions from hallucination to knotmaking to forgetfulness; moving from women laughing to a woman who eats with her fist clenched; from a vital firefly to a reborn Don Quixote to a stubborn old woman; from modern police savagery to a fantasized turkey-shoot in the days of Natty Bumppo; and ending with the poet, fishing from his heart.

In two particular ways, these new poems demonstrate how experience "bitter in thy belly" can flower into literature. The title poem obviously, and others hopefully, argue that gain. More imponderable as an oblique consequence are the haiku, forward-looking because never attempted before, undertaken to end this book, not with traditional little pictures from nature, but with "breakaway" handfuls—sometimes fistfuls—of truth remembered.

But, to quote the "Dialogue" in section V, "All of you fists are rather ugly." Although beauty hardly invests the loathing of privileged brutality that nerves "Deadly James," it is hoped that readers will feel it elsewhere here in love at first sight, roller skate girls, and flowers that pop open.

Paris, France
19 April 1987   J.A.E.

Contents

VI. Breakaway Haiku

VII. The Poet as Fisherman

"False Notions"

I. False Notions and Other Things

They know the brutal business
of my thinking;
I know they have no charity nor memory
to return the way they came

False Notions, Fears, and Other Things of Wood

Repeatedly, that sturdy stump in me
bears up like stone,
beneath some ritual I see:
the blinding axe
swings up,   holds
that moment of its weightlessness
inscrutable
till I confirm the arm is mine;
I will it, grip,
feel moist the swelling handle,
the shudder rude,
the difference fallen.

Toward that chopping block
I carry in me woodthings—
infectious undergrowth
pretending upwards
through each stem and branch of me—
all so certain of themselves
they practice, like pains,
the craft of being.

They try to wrench away
before we reach that stump,
my woodthings and I,
they   weakening
in its brightness,

in my luminously saying
"I must go, must go
to the chopping block."

They know the brutal business
of my thinking;
I know they have no charity nor memory
to return the way they came—
came not from wilderness,
nor forest,
nor living trees.

Their craft and strength I test—
    and mine—
at the chopping block.
1986   *1987*

Boxes, Trunks, and Darkness

Sliding in their skin of darkness,
they gorged his hallway to the door,
heaved   their stillness on his sleepy eye,
where he sensed them one gigantic creature
prehistoric from its head (a heavy box of tools)
to tail (long skis protruding past a trunk).

Dinosaur. . .deathlike fatigue stretched out the word
that tracked such lumpish footfalls to his bed,
shrank it back into boxes, trunks,
lay with it there in tremors, throbbing,
a heartbeat faster than a man's,
or a slower, massive one enraged.

He slightly turned (a backward motion
from the body he had made)
and, held by clockbeats near it,
drifted back two hundred million years
to rage that clawed the hills apart:
conflict too fierce to feel
till shouldergripe revived his days
among tough boxes, trunks to pack;
each choice, if sore
(whether grudgingly keep   or guiltily junk)
itself a wrath, a grief, a changeless pain
    even when—he rose on one elbow to know it—
    the decimated lot

regrouped like grim survivors,
their tight-lipped knots,
uncompromising locks
resolute to not remember,
to clench tomorrow
breathless if need be,
crossing the sea.

The darkness of it all put him to sleep, exhausted,
his dinosaur set free
to roam among its kind, unrealized
by shape, by sound, in senses plain
till claimed again by mortal memories
drilled through.
1984   *1987*

The Knotmaker

Unaware   he stepped into the trap,
dead-white kitchen cord
that angered up, it seemed, into the knot
as if some killer-current racing through it
burned   to snatch his foot,
hiss high, and dangle him
against electric oven.

Fantasy, it challenged him,
its source and sizzling logic fleshed
in his past. He plunged,
but found no lyncher's knot,
no guilty rawhide damage done;
though, climbing out, he unwound no one's tourniquet
torn from his own sleeve, his very back.

The bloodless cord arched   toward his leg
till reason eased him: "You only dropped it;
the plug's too far." "So true,"
unopened rice, pale dregs of spice
and shrinking kitchenstuff agreed.
Refrigerator door then shuddered into life,
dissent, and hummed of secret power
coiled in its dark

down where black magnet glowed
to trance his thought into the bin
where peppers, carrots, lettuce
lay in shrouds of vapory plastic,
his tight knots topping each
like bobtails wrenched—
twists unremembered by his hand
until his drifting eye found others
strangling the cupboard's innocents:
slim packs of instant coffee, toothpicks, bread.

Recognition, like a falling cup unbroken in his hand,
suspended him near knots
distorting other shelves:
the wardrobe where his hoarded, braided twine
was hanging on a nail,
the bookcase where cassettes of old-flame music

lay silent, tied up face-to-face—
more furnishings to be stomached
on his inmost rack of all,
his deepest knots,
his little gutmasters   waiting
for surprise.
1984   *1987*

Party-Pooper

Pyjama parties, come-as-you-are bashes,
then this one, on his patio,
a fairyland where stones wore colors,
lamps wore breathing skirts,
and ladies wore outlandish masquerades.

An up-and-down-the-stairs night,
his smile forecast—
costumes coming loose with hands to help,
masks and bands stretched up or down, depending.
Then SHE appeared.

A stranger, he felt, trespasser no:
her walk belonged;
she carried treasure, it would seem,
from antennas shimmering on her hair
down to headlines braided into sandals.
From slender waist to naked thighs
she wore a cardboard box
mashed and taped to simulate a globe,
the earth, its continents clipped and pasted on
from maps and airline magazines.

Bravo! he thought,
imagining his hands on Ghana and Nigeria,
slipping up to Paris and Versailles,
the magnet of those regions

pulling him toward her
until he saw them, front and rear,
linked by black bands of crepe
that crinkled these red-painted words
with every move she made:
"SAVE ME! SAVE ME!"

He stopped, reached backwards without turning;
music, as if on signal, rose, and arms danced him away.
Laughter frolicked into rumba, samba, tango, can-can,
but nobody danced with the earth
or saw her slowly disappear,
majestic through the darkness on the grass.
1986   *1987*

Left Umbrellas

That little old lady stole mine
(the clerk agreed)—
too close to me at Window 3,
hunched over her own business while minding mine,
puckered and sour as a stale lime,
like Paris sky that day.

Other umbrellas, other skies
drifted outside with me:
Canterbury Cathedral—I'd left one there in '72,
solaced by grandeur;
a series of them left me no face to blame,
their last-look images almost dry
beside some picnic throwaways in Kraków,
below a Courte-Paille luncheon chair in Angoulême,
behind a rugged airport bench in Denver,
beneath a battered taxi seat in Lagos.

My footstep slowed to change that guilty face:
better a man's, the prospect of a bigger canopy
snatched by wind and blasted to a treetop,
of spine and tines maimed in the mud,
a disappearance dear
as William gone to war.
Instead—a standstill thought declared—
she'd hide it in a hatbox,
wrapped in a grey-green scarf.

Crazy, at least eccentric, hiding umbrellas;
in the beginning less like Adam?
There was rain before that garden grew:
knowledge came wet into this world.
A left umbrella in such a tangle
some little old lady would have hidden,
minding the business
of Eve.
1986   *1987*

"Roller Skate Girl"

II. Announcements Nakedly Possible

On any summer night
it is lovely luck
to find women
laughing

Women Laughing

On my lean bed
fourth-floor rear
I rise hearing women laughing.
Their laughter, breathable,
stirs into water
the calm cobblestones in the courtyard.

I move on them
without sinking,
without leaving my bed
going down, down to them,
touching flavorsome strangers
who take me in,
learn me,
and hear me beginning.

On any summer night
it is lovely luck
to find women
laughing.
1984   *1987*

Love at First Sight (A Teenage Party)

As drumbeats raised the horn
that stretched into the air,
glances of the boy, the girl
touched one another;
shy, they saw the music climbing,
felt its scent—
as from a lightly perfumed soap
slipping perfectly
(no hands upon it)
from its silver wrapper.

Their smiles inhaled it,
balanced it
between them.

A word he almost said
upheld his share;
her portion answered,
a gesture given him
to please.

Theirs,
they took it in their arms,
this cleanliness,
and danced.
1984   *1987*

26

Roller Skate Girl

In memory she stands, my single dinner guest,
echo of my doorbell undulating
soft between her legs, a movement strange
until red roller skates she shifted on
loosened my surprise,
uncramped its brow and lip
in welcome deepened to delight
lively as Parisian air
trapped in creases of her purple sweatsuit
threadbare at both knees.

"I see you found the way."
"It took me thirty-three minutes."
Such common words keep watch
when mysteries begin—
and afterwards no word was wise or strong enough
to ride with me with her
those nights my fancy skated far
to bring back ancient sense
of how to move in caves, or dark of air,
to know by touch
the possibilities of love.

Her ride must be the key—
this thought each time flew me to her front door,
caught her still unsurprised, her skates on,
eyes calmly asking "Want the ride?"
body leaping, the moment of my grasp,

down fourteen steps
from churchyard near her door
to narrow street where stone amazement
split the shock
my hands grabbed up into her waist,
my legs stiff out
in the wake of her takeoff speed.

Each time I ride I ride
as I have never done before,
stretching to her, clinging,
sensing her hips are champions
as they move in the night,
racing the metro underground,
weaving me among the sinuous horns
of Right Bank traffic;
crossing Sébastopol my hands begin to slip,
and desperately they climb,
they squeeze her breasts;
almost apologetically they lapse upon her ribs,
holding on. "Hold on!"
her leaning shoulder says,
her hand on mine a promise,
her red wheels floating to my eyes
as in snow, in heaving water,
swelling to bubbles brushing my lips
before I gulp electric air, a strength
for skiing the curbs,

swimming the boulevards,
flying the River Seine
and the magic Isle
to reach the Latin Quarter where I live.

The muscles in her thighs
betray she thinks of turning;
tightening, I wonder (since my home is near);
our action floods its tiny space of time
with all she cannot teach,
nor I forget:
    the pull of single faces spinning past,
    aching in fingertips wanting our ride,
    yearning for Somebody's invitation—
    on paper wet even, snow-covered,
    dog-eared with stammerings. . .

Somewhere, patiently she stands
raw in the dusk:
Roller Skate Girl—
ruddy at both knees—
an announcement
nakedly possible,
an offering
fated to return.

1985   *1987*

My Lady Eats

My lady eats
with her fist clenched,
as if crumpling
a flower.

One noon my fingers
crossed the table cloth
gently
and opened hers.
Her silver-lacquered nails
said "Thanks,"
reclosing.

Politeness is like that:
a single rose, stood up,
an intuition, dressed
for staying out
when not invited in—
stirrings, mine and hers that day,
not braced enough
to crack the door.

I try it sometimes,
my speculations pulling:
perhaps one morning, noon, or night
when "sugars and spice and everything nice"
still wrapped her,

a familiar fist took off that coat
and dusted it with fear or shame or hate—
love, even.

My lady eats
with her fist clenched,
while I sit here
urgent
to offer break-in,
outfitted with a rose,
with syllables.
1986   *1987*

"What Matters: London *Times*, Page 12"

III. From Fireflies to The Queen

What matters
is the use of us,
from fireflies up to The Queen

What Matters: London *Times,* Page 12

The Queen, closing the Commonwealth Games,
took a royal salute from The Black Watch,
a fly-past from The Red Arrows.

Today, 4 August 86,
Sir Frederick Tymms turned ninety-seven,
Sir Victor Groom, eighty-eight;
two days ago a death mask sobered on Roy Cohn,
killer-counsel for Senator McCarthy;
"ruthless and indiscriminate," the *Times* recalls,
his "pursuit of communists
in the U.S. government and armed forces,"
himself at last pursued by law, disbarred,
bending to the charge of "fraud, blackmail and perjury,"
spending half a million a year,
confessing no "bank accounts, stocks or assets,"
charming when not repugnant,
commanding a badmouth obituary
terminating "He also had courage."

Twelve words for Eva Jelinek-Karl
three days ago dead
from "a long illness bravely borne"—
the same day gone from us a Hamblen, a Madeley
(these two wanting "no flowers, please"),
and a Maidment left to lie at Little Wratting Church
("Please, no mourning, by her own request").

One day earlier, Sophie Hiatt was born,

"a sister for James,"
like Christopher Wilson, two days older,
"a brother for Amy,"
both balancing
on such "delicate and dangerous territory"
as the sexual facts of their birth,
                    of their style of settling-in
(just like The Queen, Sir Frederick, Sir Victor)
if The Doctrine of the Faith clings to their hearts.
Add Roy Cohn's homosexuality "as a communist smear,"
Father Curran's curious books as a *cause célèbre*—
all this, the Sacred Congregation in Rome would say,
is moral matter for our gravest sense,
undiscussable.

What matters scientifically is the firefly,
caught swinging his summer lantern
through New England hedgerows:
all of him captured,
in the laboratory cloned,
his beauty crossbred into some fragile stem
startlingly to grow into a plant
new to cameras, to men,
its inner being naked, aglow,
for the first time public.

What matters
is the use of us,
from fireflies up to The Queen.
1986   *1987*

Tracks, for a Bourgeois Woman

In Alpine snow,
cross-country skis uneasily at rest
to imitate the guide,
she looked back suddenly, surprised to feel
the downward mountain pulsing in her eyes:
"a mystical experience"
(Wordsworth himself had said),
this blank-ribbed spectre
widening into her past
foundationless as sky whirled upside down—
only clouds to slow her feet,
no gripping path
except the dimly rutted trail behind them,
its whiteness rearranged by bluer air.

A trance-like quiet
palmed away her friend's bright talk
from filmy space the guide's new voice spread through
like quick-dry brushstrokes
re-coloring the portrait she had sat for
all her life:
"Perhaps you'd like," he said,
"to make tracks of your own."

The sunshine-frame of it
braced the instant
taken by her waking skis

to plunge, her willing body following,
her shining senses leaping downhill
to clinch the chance, the dare,
exhilaration blinded to the rock that rose
and jerked her headlong underneath the snow—
a trap-door disappearance, a swallowing.

Panic pushed her friend—the guide already there—
to the nothingness above her,
anxiety a shrilling vapor
until a rosy-tasseled cap,
wrenched over dripping eyes and soggy grin,
poked through the gleaming snow.

In three seconds
she had tracked a blue peak
far beyond the friendly tugs
and well-tried arm
that brushed and straightened her.

She stood up—rearranged
around her changeless core—
whisking off her mind a diamond phrase, unsaid,
about the hole she'd made,
twice her size in drawing rooms—
and deeper.
1985   *1987*

Don Quixote on the 8 O'clock News:
A View Through My Kitchen Door

The rattle of armor—
clash of my kitchen knives and battered ware—
must have roused the bearded knight:
himself on horseback (small wooden statue),
soldierly, like his sword straight out
to point the trail across my closet-top,
across its precipice, if need be,
to dare the giant eye blinked open there, turned,
and aimed from that nearby cave against him—
a new sound swelling up
(the hills, he must have proudly thought, were gathering
to watch the fray).

Quixote, pushing to attack, had not paused at a single clue:
dinnerstuff, unnoticed, lying raw,
with hands caught peeling squash at TV time
turning kitchenward the vital ray
of full-face news,
a freight of wreckage
screaming down the sky
or tumbling up in flood or fire or lava;
cooking-space at eight was the field for slaughter,
tonight from bullets, bombs, and well-dressed lies,
the body-count so high
that tarts and sauces burned.

Quixote, incensed, raised his sword,

a sword as gleaming—
though centuries had passed—
as the thought that first had driven him from home;
by itself that blade seemed riding
into the television's glare,
his battle cry a shooting star
far above the monotone of stock reports
cut short as table-time turned off the set.

Straight against that fading glow, Don Quixote rode. . .

If he should ever fall
and fail to rise,
surely the Knight of the Lions would return:
his sword come down to pierce the heart
of the utmost stone—
and tremble there,
unwrenchable
as air.
1985   *1987*

Doggerel for "Doggie" on His Birthday (for Marvin)

May you sometimes backwards be,
even when you climb a tree,
seeing new things on the ground
without the wrench of turning around;
backwards may you come and go,
letting all the gawkers know
it's not smart to look ahead
(unless you're idle, safe in bed
hoping dreams will send you clues
to find the road tomorrows use).
Backwards! backwards! is the cry
that will bring laughter to your eye.

But may you sometimes forward be,
reaching juvenility
after struggling up the track
that, if you're lucky, takes you back
to nonsense you wore on your head
instead of coverings they said
would keep you warm till comes the day
the grey bird builds his nest to stay.

Forwards! backwards! Who can tell
what will keep all Marvins well?
May you, searching, find the key
and dare to throw it into the sea.
1983   *1987*

41

An Old French Dog, Barking

The street stopped where he stood,
the sound of him cranking
like a battery dying.

Guard dog! guard dog!
The memory watered his eyes
and trailed hairlike saliva
to his toes, that trembled,
gripped the gutter like a precipice.

Precipice: the feel of it
stiffened his eighteenth-century legs
and fired his breath again
into a threatening cough.

A stylish tourist stopped
to English her pity.
"Ooooh, you babykins,"
she sighed; "him such a big, bad dog!"

His hackles translated;
his every bone and muscle
gritted to heroic sense
of what his master's voice
had countless times unleashed
to win his sleep.

He let the lady pass,
her tiptoes chastened,
while he held on mutely—
watchdog,
standing his precipice,
his post.
1986   *1987*

Flowers Pop Open

Leaning over her window boxes, pointing,
she said they would do it soon:
pop open.
The yellow ones, she meant,
flowers in her "garden"—
so she had called it, on the phone, inviting me
to come and see.

(Bus 87, believable,
had passed no pop-up flowers,
no gardens third-floor-front;
the hide-and-seek had roused in me, instead,
a thorny teenage memory
of backyard spaded up,
rich summer earth grudgingly planted,
endlessly worked.)

"Look!"
My digging faded
as her fascinated finger crooked twice,
her statue warning "Don't breathe."

Signalled by our wordlessness,
a momentary breeze arose.
Magnetic then the only flower unstirred:
a yellow one, its petals closer drawn

as if to strengthen some resolve opposed;
it kept its calyx rigid
until, perhaps, within,
the stamens, stigma, style, and ovary agreed.
Their moment come,
they softly knocked upon their upper door;
it cracked and let the evening in.
We followed with our eyes,
the colors welcoming us into their home,
motioning the guardian sepals to give way.
We saw, below, those green arms snapping out at last,
relenting, accepting the risk of contagion.

They did it:
the Mississippi burst its banks,
the lightning sprang,
the earthquake swallowed far;
and yet a lovely magic kept its promise
to the evening air:
   a flower popped open
   against all logic
   all despair.

1986   *1987*

"The Quagmire Effect"

IV. Daniel, the Crooners, and the Quagmire

He was five
and will be seven.
There is nothing under heaven
more of miracle than that

Daniel Is Six (1986)

When Daniel is six
all people should know it:
the trees show it,
the winds blow it;
nothing will be quite the same:
even Daniel's very name
will stretch and seem to make a sound
every time he writes it down
or squeezes it into the air
or combs it through his changing hair.

He was five
and will be seven.
There is nothing under heaven
more of miracle than that
except that Daniel one day sat
upon his bed and combed his hair
and dreamed of what was changing there.
1986   *1986*

The Crooners

Bing and Frank and "Mr. B,"
Como, Mathis, Eberle,
Andy, Dean, King Cole: a few
who rhymed whatever sweets
The Great Depression, war, McCarthyism
left free.

Three decades honeyvoiced the air
when crooners stopped to ask us
                 way?"
      ing
"Go   my
Hitchhikers all, we climbed aboard.
They never hurried; took time
to place a blanket on our knees
(lit up his pipe, one did, and lullabied its stem).

Once in Songland,
easy on the reins—or braking slow—
they stopped for roadside flowers
to replant around their tunes,
whistled sometimes, rat-a-tat-tatted,
low-pitched a spoken phrase or two—
their way of keeping wheels
on solid ground.
We always came back safe,

harmonizing the long notes, laughing.

Even after TV came,
they crooned right through the screen,
one hand somehow on our shoulder
when touch was needed:
lovepain too brittle to bend,
melancholy too straight from the flesh,
even the cliches marrow from our bones.

Bing, Frank, "Mr. B" and company:
old horse-and-buggy men
still singing,
taking the long road home.
1986   *1987*

The Quagmire Effect (at The Old Folks' Home)

It keeps coming back. Like yesterday.
"Cleveland Care Center": the innocent name,
the receding melancholy of the street,
should have warned me it was happening again—
The Quagmire Effect, I had gradually called it,
after Grandma died.

I remember that our bus, Old 89, grunted something
to the grey-haired driver
before their hidden overseer,
a stovepipe voice that broke all words apart,
found a singsong clarity for "STREET dem-on-stra-tions!"
then whined obscurities
that steered us down a dead end.
Old 89 just grumbled, stopped, and would not start.

We got off, one by one in search of shade,
me stepping down into a pool of August heat
flashed up so muscular, so thriving
that I blinked against it, hard and long enough
to feel again the crook of Grandma's walking stick
pinning me against the back-room door
that snowy day she found my suitcase packed.
"You just a boy," her bony finger said.
"Remember: The quagmire don't hang out no sign."

Beside the bus, her warning melted on the curb

that broke my footstep,
crisping the cool reality of my briefcase
that moved and leaned with me unknowingly
against an iron gate.

It happened then—cause and consequence
a breathlessness when "Quagmire" thickened in their place,
in my mind a blackish, wrinkled snake
sliding down around the handle of my bag,
its twin materializing upon my shoulder,
the two of them a force alive
that pulled me quickly through the gate.

Inside, a counterforce pushed back by shock:
face-to-face with me a tiny woman
old and black and straight enough
to seem the remnant of a tree
shrunken back almost to seed,
two limbs still hanging on
(I shivered, and the snakes were gone),
one to hook my briefcase,
one to draw me past the gate.

"Cleveland Care Center": the words beyond the trees,
once I saw them, might have been the signal
for cameras to grind, for everyone but me
to play a role rehearsed.
"Come on," the shrunken woman said, "and meet some folks."

"But, lady," I began, reaching for my bag.
"Young man," a feeble voice not hers was saying,
"we're mighty glad you came at last;
your mother's always tellin us bout you."

Dumbfounded, I saw my briefcase backing off
politely to make way for the new hand intercepting mine,
black and withered as the sunlit face it dangled from.
"Quagmire" oozed into my mind,
my hand as moist as hers
that crossed and clamped it.

Others moved toward me in a wavering circle:
bony arms and trembling canes,
tufted chins and watery eyes,
scalps of hair as various as blots of April snow
fading on the bottom ribs of country roads.

"This is my son, I done told you" guided my bag
that dipped and switched at instants I might speak,
might stretch for it, smiling guardedly,
hoping for a grab-all exit,
vaguely grieved that every face was black,
knowing it wasn't right—
while clasping hands with all of them
I knew it wasn't right,
and wondered what the white one hurrying toward us
was thinking.

The uniform of her big legs, milkmaid face, and nurse's cap

broke our circle,
my briefcase captive in her hand.
Her offering my bag, my taking it in silence
was affirmation binding on us all:
we swore to nothing, witnessing only
our lives joined,
a promise kept.

Sunshine in my eyes turned me away,
blindfolded me until I found the gate,
found emptiness outside: no bus, so little brawn
to hold me up against the drag of waiting.
Inside, the wait was all they had.

"Quagmire," I thought,
gripping the leather in my hand,
remembering how pleased they'd been
to see me.
1986   *1987*

"Deadly James (For All the Victims of Police Brutality)"

V. Gunhammers Cocked

The killer-cops, the San Diego three,
what made them think you deadly, James?

Deadly James (For All the Victims of Police Brutality)

The killer-cops, the San Diego three,
what made them think you deadly, James?

I take their guilty heads into my arms;
I cradle them,
my tendons hush their eyes,
illumine them to see the years roll back:
your little window, James, unsealed,
your palomino rocking horse,
his glassy eyes unquiet
when the sudden blood that splashed his ivory mane
told you the table knife you sucked on
was different, could also spit upon the tawny rug
breathtaking tracks—
deadly, James.

I embrace their heads more tightly;
their veins bulge to understand you, James,
you, hardly old enough to run,
dancing solitary in the Brooklyn rain
your older playmates dashed from,
your arms and lips and laughter reaching up
for all the sky could pour
upon the rivers capering inside you—
deadly rivers, James?

I hug their heads
with strength I had saved for you, James:

their eyeballs darken as they strain with me
to find you practicing your saxophone,
lying in the quilted heaps your bed poked up
around your stocking feet—the littered outpost
of that farther wilderness you made your room,
"NO ENTRY" blazed across the door
to guard your heartbeats
when your golden horn *believed* its one-man note—
that wild, sweet loneliness you cried—
beguiling neighbors into forgiveness
before you fumbled scales beginners know.
You   began at the top, James,
deadly.

I clasp their heads more fiercely,
empowered by the memory of you
stranded where they bled you down
into your smallest drop,
gunhammers cocked and nightsticks sinewed—
all three bewildered to find beauty
defiantly beyond them,
a tiny, dark-brown flower: the grain of you, James,
erect,
watered back to momentary life
by your manful tears.

In my iron arms their heads turn dry,
drop hollow to the ground. . .
If your new, unearthly wisdom bids you,
raise them.
But whenever you feel blood again,
or rain, or music,
pray your innocence be deadlier, James,
    much
        deadlier.

1985   *1987*

To Kill a Morning Spider

Like a thick black pencil-mark
whipped suddenly across the pinewood floor,
his blot at the bed corner
leaped to my tightening shoe,
swelled into an eight-legged coil,
oozing fur, it seemed,
angering to be recognized
as spider.

He quivered once, in a paroxysm
seized his stomach, gripped something there.
A tiny thing hopped from him, whirling—
just as my foot, clutching at itself,
smashed his eight legs.
The wheeling little thing, in pausing,
killed itself:
my shoe, an engine on its own,
crushed what was there.

Such is surprise, is destiny:
a spider in disguise,
an insect fleeing,
and we watchers from our sleep awaking
to close their being.
1986   *1987*

Dialogue Between My Fist and My Finger

"I'm more powerful than you."
"You are, but you could not say it,
    not think it, without me."
"What's that you say?"
"I said, you are nothing without me."
"But you're just a finger; I'm a fist!"
"True, but you are bent over like an old man,
    and I am straight as a new soldier."
"Your similes piss me off!"
"Your preface to your heavy book
    could have been omitted."
"You're an impertinent little bastard."
"That is because I am so relevant."
"I could get along without you, you know."
"Yes, but you would not look so handsome
    or feel so clever."
"Then you admit I'm handsome? I'm clever?"
"Only when you have me along to complement you."
"Surely you don't think I'm ugly or stupid?"
"All of you fists are rather ugly,
    and you are poorly endowed with intelligence."
"Just the same, we run every country and win every war."
"I am sorry to have joined you in either achievement."
"You sound like a 96-pound weakling.
        Where's your patriotism?"
"If I point to it, will you carry it?"

"Are you trying to get cute with me?
    I'll knock your block off!"
"You will have to maim yourself some other day:
    our body is waking up from his nap."
"I hope he wants us to knock somebody's block off!"
"If I were you. . . ."
"But you ain't me. You're just a finger. So shut up!"
1986   *1987*

A Black Militant Poem Speaks

I was born militant:
screamed
when the world first   touched me,
slapped me into life.

Measles, mumps, and scarlet fever
stalked me to school,
envied my blackboard stardom,
dragged me homeward from my inkwell
to test my fighting back.
I had battle scars at nine.

Retilo Remos taught me to curse
like Mexicans
pushed into worm-thin boxcars
(their homes   that smoked and scowled back—
cocoons across the railroad tracks),
while words my father's Blackness hated
chewed my homework pencil,
hardened my grip.

Gang-war trampled my seasons,
aging me in its schoolrooms, armies, offices, bedrooms:
the same Black lessons smearing each desk, each day, each year,
the same merciless faces reddening the mud,
the same outmaneuvered hands crumpling the memorandums,

the same passionless asses printing lies on clean linen.

At last, this voiceful hour
bursts me out of a lifelong cave,
sticks me upright and formal
among delicate eavesdroppers,
my brittle memories the strength,
the need,
to lift this   club
in my hands.
1985   *1987*

My First Novel, Page One

SHOWDOWN IN TURKEYTOWN, I named it,
absurd, cornmealish as the subtitle,
"Americana Digged Out";
wrote faster, stationed experts on the firing-line
I had imagined on seeing them real on TV,
tough-minded on armament every one at the table,
potbellied, bemedalled, straight-backed for the conference,
trading gun-barrel reflections.

Up against Leatherstocking,
would they shine
in a turkey-shoot?

Tumbled by my eye, they landed on page one,
on Natty Bumppo's prairie turf,
the parchment target raised high by an old Indian,
their signal to fire inaudible in the fusillade.
The target tender spaced his tribal intonation well:
"No . more . room . in . bull's . eye."

Musketry and smoke and expertise
powwowed for one second,
joined by stealthy movements from the trees;
then bullets, arrows, spears,
knives, darts, a tomahawk or two,
slingshot pebbles, spitballs—

all *thukked* or *fit* or *splut*
with deadeye certainty.

Everything in range, fair game,
gave up its target-tidbit,
pierced and cut and chopped and knobbed,
raw to the fact that experts had arrived.

Nothing fleshed out, in Turkeytown,
after page one.
1986   *1987*

Firing Squads

Firing squad,
metal-lipped, and blind to what they see,
rifle sights pointed like testimony
cut up, regrooved, tooled into line,
trigger fingers light as veins
coiled in a clock stopped ticking—
dirtywork draftees
fertilizing the flag.

Firing squad,
proud as the Arlington bugler,
shining their boots for the burial,
shooting salutes to the grieving air:
bullets for the hero
still soldiering there.

Firing squad,
bandoliered, bearded as mountain shrubbery,
scowling at barefoot traitors
    tongue-tied at the thought of treason,
    roped against ancestral trees,
    jerking at last like rag dolls
    dead-tired of it all.

Firing squad bedamned—
if it be possible
to damn the daily business
of this world.
1986   *1987*

"For France, IV (Françoise)"

VI. Breakaway Haiku

Indians, cowboys
crossed my town with faces brown
like rocks. They were real.

Breakaway Haiku

For Midwestern Boys:

I

Indians, cowboys
crossed my town with faces brown
like rocks. They were real.

II

Sticks, I called my horse.
I painted him, rode him hard.
His grave is secret.

III

He took turpentine,
knife, and pail—"to nut the pigs,"
he called it. I learned.
1986   *1987*

Breakaway Haiku

For Hard Times:

I

From laths in our walls
we ripped winter wood to burn.
Our landlord was poor.

II

Hot bricks in the bed,
wrapped in rags too torn to wear,
kept my sisters warm.

III

From tall ten-cent bags,
day-old pastries for the poor,
I filched going home.

IV

Slick magazine strips
rolled slim around coffee grounds
made smokes in those days.

1986   *1987*

Breakaway Haiku

For a Depressed Woman:

I

My friends do not know.
But what could my *friends* not know?
About what? What friends?

II

She sleeps late each day,
stifling each reason to rise,
choked into the quilt.

III

"I'll never find work."
She swallows this thought with pills,
finds tears in the glass.
1986   *1987*

Breakaway Haiku

For France:

I (French Boy)

A beanstalk of bread,
cooling sideways behind him,
bicycled him home.

II (Three-Star View)

Mont-Saint-Michel rose
into my windshield, held me
tight against the wheel.

III (Pétanque)

Toothless, bending low,
his sixty years of practice
spun the ball. He smiled.

IV (Françoise)

He sells no paintings,
Françoise in her summer slacks
stretching to kiss him.
1986   *1987*

Breakaway Haiku

For Racists Remembered:

I

"For White Only" was
what they meant, no matter what
pie was being sliced.

II

They cursed at children,
murdered, cleaned their hands with laws.
Strong people fought back.

III

Their greetings mocked us:
Rastus, Sambo, Shine—and boy.
Men they did not greet.

IV

We said "Sir" sometimes:
"Sir Charles," "Sir Honkie," and then
the big lie: "the Man."
1986   *1987*

"Poet as Fisherman"

VII. The Poet as Fisherman

Oh, I have tried the moon, thermometers—
the bait and time and place all by the rule—
fishing for the masterpiece

Poet as Fisherman

I fish for words
to say what I fish for,
half-catch sometimes.

I have caught little pan fish flashing sunlight
(yellow perch, crappies, blue-gills),
lighthearted reeled them in,
filed them on stringers on the shore.
A nice mess, we called them,
and ate with our fingers, laughing.

Once, dreaming of fish in far-off waters,
I hooked a two-foot carp in Michigan,
on nylon line so fine
a fellow-fisher shook his head:
"He'll break it, sure; he'll roll on it and get away."
A quarter-hour it took to bring him in;
back-and-forth toward my net,
syllable by syllable I let him have his way
till he lay flopping on the grass—
beside no other, himself enough in size:
he fed the three of us (each differently)
new strategies of hook, leader, line, and rod.

Working well, I am a deep-water man,
a "Daredevil" silver wobbler
my lure for lake trout in midsummer.

Oh, I have tried the moon, thermometers—
the bait and time and place all by the rule—

fishing for the masterpiece,
the imperial muskellunge in Minnesota,
the peerless pike in Canada.
I have propped a well-thumbed book
against the butt of my favorite rod
and fished from my heart.

Yet, for my labors,
all I have to show
are tactics, lore—
so little I know
of that pea-sized brain I am casting for,
to think it could swim
with the phantom-words
that lure me
to this shore.
1986   *1987*

ABOUT THE AUTHOR

Reared in Nebraska, working on ranches and farms, James A. Emanuel had jobs in Colorado, Kansas, and Iowa before his Washington, D.C. post at twenty as Confidential Secretary to the USA's first Black general, Benjamin O. Davis, Sr., the Assistant Inspector General of the Army. After overseas duty as a 93rd Infantry staff sergeant, he earned degrees from Howard and Northwestern Universities and married in Chicago.

His long career as a teacher in the USA and abroad started at the Harlem YWCA Secretarial School and, after his Ph.D. from Columbia, at The City College of The City University of New York, where he introduced the study of Black poetry in 1966. In 1968 he was awarded an invitational Fulbright lectureship at the University of Grenoble, France, and in 1975 a similar post at the University of Warsaw, Poland. Before and after the latter, he was given teaching positions at the University of Toulouse, including a professorship on the French National Contingent. He retired from teaching in 1984.

Twenty-five or more reference books identify Emanuel's main literary works. Critics have recently examined his life as a poet in *La Rive Noire: De Harlem à la Seine* (1985), *Afro-American Poets Since 1955* (1985), and *Caliban* (1986), a bilingual Toulouse publication. He has detailed his European experiences, often with photographs, in his manuscript *Snowflakes and Steel*, on archival deposit at Duke University.

His best-known prose books did pioneer service *(Langston Hughes* in 1967 and *Dark Symphony: Negro Literature in America* in 1968); and his reading his poetry, available in well over a hundred anthologies, led to his wide travels in Europe, Africa, and the USA. He now considers himself "only a poet," increasingly involved in translations of his work.

ABOUT THE ILLUSTRATOR

The cover and internal illustrations were created by Nicole Lamotte, an often-decorated French painter and sculptor (she has the coveted *Médaille d'argent de la ville de Paris*) who is internationally known for her unique style "on the brink of both surrealism and symbolism" and for her numerous exhibitions, one of the notable ones permanently at the celebrated Galerie Katia Granoff in Paris.

ABOUT THE AUTHOR'S POEMS:
A SELECTED CHRONOLOGY OF COMMENTARY

1974: He is "among the best" of those Black authors "writing a vital poetry that promises much for the future." (Donald Barlow Stauffer in *A Short History of American Poetry*)

1977: "Emanuel seems destined to become one of the major Black poets." (Ann Semel and Kathleen Mullen in *Black American Poetry: A Critical Commentary*)

1979: One cannot mistake "the urgency of the voice....the authenticity....which, in converging with his technique of undertones, produces the remarkable intensity....provides the key to what Stephen Henderson has aptly called the 'lucid, confident strength in James Emanuel.'" (Marvin Holdt in *Black American Literature Forum*)

Emanuel, "a true poet" without doubt, "weaves his tapestry from human frailties, from hidden places of pain and joy, prejudice and love." (Joe Weixlmann in *Black American Literature Forum*)

1982: "Emanuel orders sometimes stark views with almost a lawyer's sense of 'rules of evidence' and a quiet humor." (Gene Fowler in *Home Grown Books*)

1985: His "keen, sensitive perceptions of youth and love and heart-rending images of pain and racial oppression" make him "an indispensable figure in black American poetry." (Douglas Watson in *Afro-American Poets Since 1955*)

His poems "proposent des moments ou des êtres chers au coeur du poète et qui, dans l'abolition des différences raciales et nationales, sont tout simplement humains et amicaux." (Michel Fabre in *La Rive Noire: De Harlem à la Seine*)

1986:   He "links with the recent preoccupations of several current major French writers,...Marguerite Duras, Philippe Sollers, and more especially Alain Robbe-Grillet...." (Anthony Suter in *Caliban*)

1987:   "James Emanuel apparâit ici comme *poète de l'instant*; de l'instant immédiat ou remémoré, disseque, analyse, illustré de métaphores assez expressionnistes; de l'instant...évocateur de souvenirs cruels ou source de douloureuses leçons." (Jean Migrenne, translator of this volume and earlier poems)